The Great Cape

A fable about effecti

By Derek Robertson

Chartered FCIPD, MCMI, MInstLM, NLP Practitioner & Coach

Foreword by Henry McLeish, First Minister of Scotland, 2000-2001

Cover illustration

Vizibility Digital, Stirling

What people say about SÜPERB Meetings™

"Great mix of resources, examples, and tools to use in a variety of situations."

sportscotland

"Great programme. I now understand how to create a more engaging and effective meeting."

"This was a great programme. I learnt a lot from this, and would recommend it to all."

People's Postcode Lottery

"Found it very useful; I attend and hold meetings, some of which are less than motivational. I have lots of tools and awareness to do things differently now."

"Very relevant to our day-to-day job. Lots of useful tips to apply straight away."

The Scottish Salmon Company

"Training has given me the tools to have fulfilling meetings."

"I will use the techniques from today in my day-to-day work."

Charles River Laboratories

"This training has been very useful in showing us what we were doing wrong, and has demonstrated the benefits of good practices."

Scottish Development International, Paris office

"All excellent. Lots of fun and enlightening participation with lots of helpful strategies."

"I'm going to put into practice what I have learnt, especially planning."

Scottish Enterprise

Contents

Dedication

I dedicate this fable to a great friend, Ally Dudgeon. The universe took his light from us far too soon. He was so funny and kind hearted. He knew how to balance having a life and working hard. Above all, he genuinely lit up a room with his presence.

I was drafting this book in Tenerife when I got news of his death. A freak road traffic accident did the deed. There is only one loser when a car at speed hits a cyclist. The image of his cheeky face reciting Monty Python skits word for word was my constant companion as I wrote. Maybe he was looking over my shoulder?

Acknowledgements

I have a lifetime in business and people development, with an enduring fundamental belief that engaged people do great things. I'd love to list all the positive influences on me, but I'll have to prioritise. To Theresa Schneider who opened my eyes to people development, supported my ideas to get qualified and improve myself, and got out of the way to let me apply what I'd learned. To Sarah Aubrey who invested huge trust in me to design programmes of over a million words. Finally, Elaine McGinn, the most astute, pragmatic, and down-to-earth high-achieving senior manager I've ever come across. I've left every meeting with her, laden with reflections and actions. It's these kinds of leadership that created the conditions for me to do probably my best work, often under immense time pressures.

In getting the book to this stage, I'd mention these folks: Ian Dudgeon (Ally's brother) who added ideas to the prose; John Cross and Frances Ainslie who reviewed early drafts, causing me to rethink the structure and content; Scott Dickson, Anna Bell, and Craig McClure who added their insights; and always remembering my wife, Jane, and daughter, Elaine, who put up with me during the development process of bringing this production to life.

Foreword

The world of meetings

By Henry McLeish. Scotland's First Minister 2000 -2001

After 50 years of public service, including 30 years of being elected, I am a true veteran of, 'meetings', in every sense of that word. And for good measure I come from the more discerning, some would say sceptical, maybe even cynical view of what my involvement in thousands of meetings has achieved, for me, my electors, and my country. I do stop short of John Kenneth Galbraith's view that, "meetings are indispensable when you don't want to do anything", and the American writer, Thomas Sowell who said, "people who enjoy meetings should not be in charge of anything". My enduring assessment arrived at after decades of meetings was simply, why do we have so many of them?

Based on my own experiences, I was surprised and delighted to read Derek Robertson's new book, 'The Great Cape Escapade-A fable about effective meetings'. An excellent vehicle for telling a short story about general truths, this fable has humour, and is insightful, informed and so uncannily accurate about the psychology and dynamic of meetings, the conduct and behaviour of people attending and the myriad of different characters and motivations that exist.

The fable's hero, Dakkc (pronounced Dax) and the story, may be light years away, but the issues raised are real and topical. Derek Robertson is an award-winning HR professional and combines a wide range of experience and expertise, with an unshakeable faith in the ability of meetings to be 'consistently fulfilling'. His mission is to persuade us of this piece of wisdom.

Derek makes many important points, which I certainly agree with. First, when senior people chair meetings, it will block feedback. Second, organisations do not treat participants or Chair roles as skills. Third, the delusion that meetings cannot be improved. When you consider the extraordinary number of meetings that are held, it is remarkable that formats and frequency and routine and results are rarely questioned. The holding of the meeting itself can often be the outcome!

And you will recognise the characters and tactics that Derek identifies. The hidden agenda, the speech maker, the higher grade, the not-commenting and the over-zealous and silent scribes, who never contribute, but just take notes-not the minutes- to lock away for useful encounters in the future.

Talking about characters, I learned decades ago one of the most important lessons of a long political life. Before being elected to Westminster, myself, along with a group of senior councillors from Scotland, attended a meeting in London with the Government Minister responsible for the Oil industry. Oil was big in Scotland in the 70's and 80's and our mission was to issue our demands and allow the minister adequate time to be impressed and give us the answers we were looking for.

It did not turn out that way. We were so full of our own importance and enjoyed the sound of our own voices that we lost focus. The Minister said we had an hour before his next meeting and asked us to outline our concerns. For the next fifty-nine minutes each of us in turn used the meeting as a stage and went on and on and on. We tripped the ego switch.

At one minute to noon, the Minister rose to his feet thanked us for coming and said he had listened carefully, and then left. We had gained nothing. Out manoeuvred. And speechless. A well-conceived strategy had been clinically delivered. We had been hoisted with on our own petard!

This exercise in naivety taught me a great deal about 'meetings'!

Derek Robertson has written a readable and helpful book on a subject most people would regard as difficult to digest, and too dry for an easy read. But, Derek's thoughtful analysis, enlivened by humour, relevant to our contemporary world, and with an out of our earth and optimistic apprentice Dakkc, makes the book work.

Remaining a sceptic, I thought the 2020 Coronavirus Pandemic and the subsequent work at home guidance would have seen the demise of the meeting, but I had underestimated the relentless onward drive of technology and the emergence of, Zoom, and the virtual meeting. Maybe it is too early to judge whether this enhanced technology will help ease some of the universal criticisms of meetings or merely add further to the paranoia created when people are physically separated and it becomes harder for them to judge what people are really getting up to!

After reading Derek's book many readers will see meetings in a completely different light and take comfort from the idea that they can be 'consistently fulfilling'.

My conversion on the road to Dakkc's home world of Süperbania, is not yet complete but I remain now in the land of the sceptics with cynicism fast receding into interplanetary space.

Throughout my life of meetings, there is one small issue of significance where I am proud to claim some success. In most meetings there is an item, "AOCB". Any-meaningless, Other-meaningless and extensive, Competent-because it is consistent with ancient rules and regulations from a bygone age, or even worse the Chair's judgement, and Business- defined as a usually commercial or mercantile activity engaged in as a means of livelihood. I have made progress by banishing such an item from meetings which I have chaired. It is not a big ask but surely it will not be part of an inter galactic extension of the meeting or be part of an expansion of Zoom to the universe.

This is a good read, a fable of significance, that will change views and create a new set of meetings skills that can be identified and nurtured to the benefit of the millions of decisions that are taken on our behalf as citizens, and consumers. Long overdue, but to be honest Derek it would have been more useful to me half a century ago!

About the Author

Derek Robertson is the meetings guy. Born and raised in historic Bannockburn, central Scotland, his DNA's coated in a land of thinkers, creatives, and patriots. People who challenged, persevered, and changed the way things were: often taking great personal risks along the way. From his house, he sees the iconic Stirling Castle and the monument to Sir William Wallace (remember Braveheart?). He often walks the nearby field of Robert the Bruce's 1314 victory for independence. These, and more, influence his passion, tenacity, and ability to challenge the status quo.

He's an award-winning HR professional and a disciple of accelerated learning. His people- development philosophy is crushingly simple: "Engaged people do great things." This underpins his world-class, simple, creative, and enjoyable training programmes. His alumni boasts over seventy thousand participants from more than fifty countries.

The passion for consistently fulfilling meetings came from countless training participants sharing their meeting frustrations. Regardless of country, three themes appeared. Firstly, the tendency for the most senior person to chair meetings. This creates a block to feedback and challenge. Secondly, organisations don't treat participant or chair roles as core skills. That means people learn meeting behaviours from what they observe, and if those behaviours are not good... Thirdly, there's a global delusion that meetings just can't be improved.

Derek's driven to fix that. Meetings are an obvious source of easy bottom-line benefit. He argues that every organisation seeking high performance must first create a solid foundation. That means achieving consistently fulfilling meetings, strong email management, and focused use of time.

The motivation to write this book was to start a conversation: to get people talking, and sharing their meetings' experiences and good practice. The book is a contribution, however big or small, to changing this one aspect of the business world.

He has a huge interest in storytelling, and believes it's such a powerful way to engage people. That makes it a great learning method. The seeds of publishing something accessible as a story began to germinate in 2010. The fable idea then took root, grounded in his massive interest in movies, sci-fi, and Monty Python. Like the Giant Himalayan lily, that flowers every seven years, the manuscript lay dormant in a hard drive for a similar time. Thankfully, it's now blossomed out of the COVID-19 pandemic of 2020.

All of us, like movie heroes, aspire to something better but doubt whether we've got what it takes. It's unlikely we'll see Luke Skywalker or Katniss Everdeen ever chair a meeting, so Derek created Dakkc (pronounced Dax) as the protagonist who is challenged, but longs to succeed.

Derek knows first-hand that people who use his array of materials and tools improve their meetings, and their meeting participants love them for it.

Introduction

Chair consistently effective meetings and you'll join us in improving the world. You'll guarantee your heroic status with everyone, from your co-workers all the way to your CEO. They'll love you. Chair them badly, and you become a carrier of the 'ineffective meetings disease'. You'll contribute to all the associated cost, frustration, poor decisions, and harm to your personal and organisational brand health.

My conviction is that we (the global business community) are already infected. We settle for unfulfilling and ineffective meetings. They're an enormous waste of time, money, and energy.

Our company had 'trained' people in the usual way for years (albeit with a great course). We've spoken to thousands about meetings in what's become thirty-five years of market research. Today, our continuing mission is for great meetings' practice across our planet. One that'll make us the envy of the universe. I reflect that all my working life may have led to this vocation and to our ever-growing suite of themed practical support to promote consistently fulfilling meetings.

To warm people up to the topic, or as simply a great way to learn, I welcome you to the fable.

Using a story lets you look at meetings' practice in a detached way. While you enjoy the read, I'm sure you'll recognise the meeting situations that appear. More than this, you'll surely identify with our hero's journey of change. The story happens many light years from here, but the issues are close, personal, and real.

Squeeze the most from the book

I've put prompt questions at the end of each chapter. I'd encourage you to make your own scribbles, reflections, and, of course, actions.

So prepare your favourite drink, relax into your favourite chair, and enjoy the ride.

Let's jump to light speed.

Derek Robertson

Well Hello to You

4-D date 07-01

Welcome. I'm Dakkc. (For species with just the one tongue, you pronounce it Dax.) My publishers tell me that I've made such a big bang across a host of galaxies, that there's been a hullabaloo to publish my personal logs of the time. I welcome you to what became the greatest of times for me, my home world of Süperbania, and potentially every planet.

My logs describe my coming of age project: my passage from apprentice to hero. In short, the better the project delivery, the better the heroic capability our Guardians bestow. I longed to do well. My father's coming of age hadn't inspired. He got the minor heroic title of 'Doughmakerman'. It draped him with the ability to make great bread products, plus an annoying extra ability to talk nonstop about his super-power. My grandmother, 'Sewagewoman', wasn't much of a role model either. I yearned in my three guts for more.

Anyhow, to help you, I've used your timescales instead of our 'rotations'. We don't have male or female, so we live in relative harmony. Jemst, my absolute best friend, and I randomly assigned a gender to the players in my odyssey.

Finally, you should know that our Guardians authorised us for fourth-dimension travel (4-D). This makes light speed look like a slug on an *Aergian* cabbage.

So, let's go back to the start and find out about my passage project.

Dakkc's Log: My Project
4-D date 62-78

Today felt like a fateful one. Master Al Geon, the wisest of our race (still in physical form), and I met at her retirement home. (I'll refer to the Master as she/her for your understanding. I don't know why the she strikes me as having female traits, but then again, the Master does have an obsession with footwear.) We met to go over my passage project. I still can't believe the Master took such an interest in my project. She did, though, slip into the conversation that she knew my father and believed in him—until the dark side of biscuit-making and cookie-dough corrupted him.

My audience seemed to last an eon. Maybe because I felt so overwhelmed. After all, Master Al Geon took the time to brief ME!

I'm to chair Project Enlighten's planning meetings. The project is Süperbania's first contact with the Blue Planet. The Blue Planet is in the one-star system, and an intelligent species made mostly of water populate it. I say intelligent loosely. Jemst says they're capable of great beauty and creativity but at the same time they're also barbaric and cruel.

It's all so exciting. I can hardly contain myself. I plucked up the courage to ask Master Al Geon's advice about what makes a great meeting chair. She sagely encouraged me to make sure all the group members, drawn from across

Süperbania, fully understood the project and each meeting's purpose. Other than that, she told me: "Do what you think best." I got the impression that she feels meetings aren't such a great thing. A bit like the painful hives on *Ichee-Alpha*; you suffer dreadfully as you acclimatise to their atmosphere, and then you seem to just get used to them.

I'm a little perplexed, though. On the one hand, Master Al Geon showed great interest in me, but on the other hand, I felt the Master's resignation that I'll only be satisfactory. Unlikely to rock the world, and just as unlikely to cause an extinction level event, such as my grandmother's in the great sewage catastrophe of *Vayu*.

Maybe it was remembering *Vayu's* polluted oceans that prompted her to prattle on about horseshoe crabs. I thought she was having a senior moment! Apparently they're living fossils on Süperbania and many other worlds. "Special," she called them. "Ignored by many yet they possess special gifts." Aside from having many eyes and blue blood, it is impossible for them to get cancer. Looking evermore sleepy, she mumbled, "So at some point, every planet may figure out the purpose of these magnificent creatures of potential." I politely made my excuses and left.

I'm elated to be given a project that'll secure my full heroic status. I'll get the cape I've longed for since childhood, I'll beat the odds and others' perceptions of me, and I'll restore some pride to my beleaguered family.

My soul yearns for this, and I know my answer is success with Enlighten.

My friends and other apprentices mostly wished me well. I overheard some sniping about my project team consisting of only high-achieving heroes. One said that I got this 'easy' project because my second cousin twice removed is the head chef at Master Al Geon's retirement condo—he keeps the Master supplied with her favourite *doppleberry* jello. At the same time, others said I was in for a fall as it was such a tough project. Go figure.

Later, at StarCredits over a *Tiri* expresso, some actual heroes regaled me with tales of how tricky meetings can be. They spoke of no agendas, heroes talking over the top of one another, and going over old decisions. It was nice of them. I reassured them, however, that I knew all the heroes on my project and that they were all nice. I'd be fine.

I've put much of my friends' comments down to sour *lixnicks*: not worth another moment's thought. After all, Enlighten's priority is its technical challenges. The meetings are the easy part.

My truest friend, Jemst, embraced me. She counselled me to make eye contact with every meeting participant within the first few seconds. "It helps build rapport," she said. I'd never heard of rapport. Apparently it's about connecting with people on an unconscious level; a bit like our thought-calls but without the need for H_2O hydration afterward.

Jemst did a Blue Planet college project. She's studied the 'mostly water beings', and knows lots about their sayings and customs. She'll be so helpful.

Father echoed the sense I got from Master Al Geon about meetings. He carped that they were just a downside of looking after heroes and project work. "A necessary evil," he said. He encouraged me to focus on the project team's carbohydrate intake, followed up quickly by a pastries and croissants discount offer. Father just can't resist a potential sale.

I'm so thankful for my other great mate, Non-Directive Coach. We all call him NDC. He's from *Kwezteon*, and so has many special gifts. One of them is the ability to record anything—by this I mean anything in time, space, and 4-D reality—and play it back in any format. Like the time he recorded the first Blue Planet's 'mostly water being' visit their single moon. NDC intercepted the transmission and, for a giggle, edited the words spoken. We often chuckle over the consequences had NDC not dubbed in the words 'One small step for man, one giant leap for mankind' over the original 'Wheeeeeee, man! I like, totally feel like a big balloon, man! This is totally far out!' I love NDC's sense of humour.

He's got another incredible power. He can help any sentient being achieve clarity and commitment to actions. NDC offered to help whenever I need him. I thanked him kindly, of course. I don't expect to need him because I know all the project Enlighten team, and they're all really nice.

15

Instead, we booked a friendly game of *harrouu*. (*Harrouu* is much like the Blue Planet's golf. *Harrouu* doesn't, though, have the garish clothing or the need to recount every moment of every shot to anyone who makes eye contact.) It's been great to relax with NDC after such an exciting day.

Your reflections

What do you yearn for in meetings you chair?

Dakkc has Jemst. Who do you have in your corner to help you achieve things?

My truest friend, Jemst, counselled me to make eye contact with every meeting participant within the first few seconds. "It helps build rapport,"

What advice would you give someone about to chair meetings for the first time?

Dakkc's father said meetings were, *just a downside of looking after heroes and project work.*

What's your opinion of meetings?

Dakkc's Log: First Enlighten Meeting

4-D date 62-82

Oh-My-Supreme-Celestial-Inter-Galactic-Deity! What have I done?

I've just made the biggest mistake of my short 276-year life.

Disaster! I've not witnessed such a catastrophe since the Society for Slugs, Snails and Gastropods made the fateful decision to hold their annual conference on *Briny-10*. Every hero knows that planet's surface is made of rock-salt. The whole event dissolved into one big sloppy mess—just like my first meeting.

Why is it that when you bring beings together for a meeting—even the nicest, most experienced heroes with many years of experience—they see it as an excuse to act like exhibits in an exotic menagerie where visitors overfeed sugared treats to the greater-trunked *trumpetadores*?

Today was my 'Welcome to the real world, Dakkc!' Who exactly did I think I was?

Today was Project Enlighten's first meeting, with heroes I thought were my friends. And, crikey, did I get a life lesson! With the stakes so high for me, it's no wonder I feel so bad; like the lambs of *Palioxis* that can detect the scent of mint sauce half a light year away.

And when I think back just a few days, I see that I'm such a naive apprentice hero. I mean, my earlier personal log from 62-78 was filled with optimism for the project and my burning mission to overcome my poor genes and succeed. Now I feel so worthless it hurts.

Jemst tried to get in touch. I avoided her.

I'm just too despairing to commit to this log just now. It's all too raw.

Your reflections

I've just made the biggest mistake of my short 276-year life.

What helps you when a 'meeting disaster' strikes?

Why is it that when you bring beings together for a meeting they see it as an excuse to act like exhibits in an exotic menagerie where visitors overfeed sugared treats to the greater-trunked trumpetadores?

What's the biggest lesson you've learned in meetings?

I'm just too despairing to commit to this log just now. It's all too raw.

What does Dakkc need right now?

Dakkc's Log: Impotent
4-D Date 62-82

… I've returned to this log. I've had a chance to relax a bit with the help of a *Hypnosian* chill pill. I now want to commit my thoughts on this, my rude awakening.

I did some things well today. For our first meeting, I brought home-made pastries. (Although I didn't, need my father's detailed description of dough folding that makes a *Demeter*-Danish so flaky!) I did it to show that I, too, am a nice hero. I followed Master Al Geon's advice, and spent lots of energy on making sure that everyone knew, in glorious 4-D, the project's purpose. I also made eye contact within the opening seconds, as Jemst suggested. Every one of them smiled back at me. That was the last time I felt good at today's first meeting.

Noting my full disaster list would, as Jemst would say, put the hyper-monkeys of *Aergia* to sleep, so I'll limit this to a summary:

- The meeting didn't start or finish on time.
- Higher-Grade arrived late (though he did say "Sorry").
- My agenda was poor.
- There was jargon I hadn't heard before.
- We had discussions that seemed to go round and around like the thirteen moons of *Un-Luhkey Alpha*.

- My 'nice' heroes behaved badly, with me powerless to stop it.
- Actions, such as I managed, were vague.

I feel so dejected. Impotent. Maybe I really am no better than my ancestors. At one point—during the meeting!—I was negotiating with myself to give up my bid for hero status. "Perhaps," I pondered, "I should settle for continuing my physical existence as it was. After all, cookie dough is a valuable commodity in some galaxies, and joining the family firm may not be so bad." I even heard myself muse, "A cape only adds to my cleaning debits anyway" and "I'd rather not progress than be renamed with something worse than Granny Sewagewoman."

As I clipped my toenails whilst watching the nightly reruns of *Intergalactic* Friends, I contemplated going to Master Al Geon to quit. It was so weird that our wisest of beings thought-called me at just that moment.

She talked a little in riddles. At one point she referred to those horseshoe crabs again, and then about my ... destiny? I thought that the Master may have had too many after-dinner *Dionysian* port wines. I'm just chairing planning meetings. My 'destiny' is taking things a bit too far. After hydrating with some H_2O, I waded through her meanderings.

Her wisdom's thrust was that poor meetings were an unfortunate part of life. Sure, I could develop one or two little tricks but essentially, unfulfilling meetings are inevitable—rather like wrinkles and cellulite. Pleased that Master Al Geon had been in touch, but not really helped by her, I looked to Jemst, my longest and truest friend.

Jemst arrived after ten. We watched a romantic comedy in 4-D starring Cain Mogenisti clone IX and, returning from cryogenic thawing, Dawn Harryless. He smells great as an actor, and she is so cute. Just as we finished our *Demeter* pizza with noodle beer, father called.

He consoled me with "What did you expect?" followed by a generous helping of its close relative, "I told you so". He only pushed me closer to settling for making the best of what's now going to be a trial. It's sure losing is lustre as the adventure I thought it was.

Jemst simply listened to me as I talked ... and talked ... and talked.

Maybe a good night's sleep will help.

Your reflections

I did some things well today.

> What is done consistently well at meetings in your world?

I spent lots of energy on making sure that everyone knew, in glorious 4-D, the project's purpose.

How well do you make sure participants know every meeting's purpose?

Which items on Dakkc's summary disaster list can you identify with?

Master Al Geon stated that 'poor meetings were an unfortunate part of life'. What do you think your senior leaders think about meetings?

Dakkc's Log: The Plan

4-D date 69-01

Saved! ... I think.

Jemst came around early. She's changed my life force today. I'd been contemplating hero career suicide, and an existence settling for what was clearly going to include unfulfilling and stressful meetings. Jemst sat me down, then quietly and clearly set me straight.

She began with four words: "I believe in you." Then she posed a question, "Can you believe in yourself?" Before I had a chance to answer, she asked me to trust my three guts, that everything worth doing needs effort, and that I had plenty of people and help around me. She told me that to be successful, I would need to Think, Plan, Do. She said it was simple, and that many Blue Planeters use it as a mantra. After all, even they can't forget three things.

She went on, "Heroes will tell you things, give their opinions, and even infect you with their hang-ups. Your job is to think. Think about what you want, what you know, and what you feel. Some advice you'll use; others you'll decide not to. The point is that you will have followed the plan. Think, Plan, Do; Think, Plan, Do; Think, Plan, Do."

Just as I was getting my head, and three guts, around Jemst's plan, NDC arrived. NDC helped me get perspective. Some practical actions came squarely to the front and centre. So squarely that I almost got a nosebleed!

He helped me appreciate the good things I did, including preventing father from giving the participants his infamous top-ten whisking techniques demo. More seriously though, NDC also helped me to realise that:

- The participants were simply being themselves— even nice heroes need boundaries
- Pastries are nice, but me behaving like a country club host—being everyone's friend—isn't a route to high performance
- I need to control heroes' contributions so that each one is timely, relevant, and valuable
- Builder and Creative didn't speak at all, and I need to address that
- Speech-Maker talked too much, and lots of it didn't add anything
- I got so nervous, that I skipped over the rules and roles like a *sonzi* beast from the Kinkard mountains bounds over *clarp* nettles
- Details' minutes arrived like the transcript from the courtroom drama, 'Twelve Angry Heroes'. I'd assumed we'd get key points and an action list.

Using NDC's special gift, we reviewed one meeting excerpt. It gave classic proof of my chairing naiveté.

> Me: And so to rules and roles. I think it will help us, and ultimately the Blue Planet Project Enlighten, to agree our meeting rules and roles. In

other words, what do we need to do together to make this a productive set of meetings? Who has a suggestion?

Not-Committed: Yes, Dakkc. Your enthusiasm is commendable—really it is. I'm impressed. When I look around the room, though, I see others like me, veterans of meetings over many years. We all know how they work. Let's just crack on with the agenda, and I'm sure we can keep you right.

Me: Well, eh ... eh, thanks ... eh, Not-Committed ... I think. I wanted a Success Contract, really. It'll help us be more efficient and effective. That's why ... eh ... eh ... I was ... eh ... keen to work on it together ..."

Hidden-Agenda: Dakkc, I don't want to stop you mid-sentence, but I have to agree with Not-Committed here. This is your first project, yes? Well, I would say that in this room there's probably over a thousand years' experience. We're ready to get down to the agenda now, so why don't we get going?

Me: Well ... eh ... if you think it best ... eh ... let's try that shall we?

What a failure. As unplanned as the attempted repopulation of the mosquito-infested *Atar-4* without barrier cream, and as naive as a seven-headed *acneid* from *Hades-Beta* entering a beauty pageant.

And Higher-Grade arrived late.

So, whilst there are lots of faults and things that I need to think about, NDC helped me get to firm actions—ones I can do.

I've decided that I'm not going to settle for my meeting lot. No. I will not. Of course, it'll be scary for me, but I have the Think, Plan, Do mantra. I can now see an opportunity to be better. I'll use NDC, Master Al Geon, Jemst, any hero, and anything that'll help me. By the next *nexus eclipse*, which will be around the end of Project Enlighten, I WILL be the chair of a high-performing team—and damn those horseshoe crab thingies.

I believe in myself. Not fully yet, but enough to commit.

Your reflections

Jemst sat me down, then quietly and clearly set me straight.

> Who can you rely on to talk with you honestly, openly, and directly? If you have someone, thank them; if you don't, why not find someone?

Details' minutes arrived like the transcript from the courtroom drama, 'Twelve Angry Heroes'. I'd assumed we'd get key points and an action list.

Are your meeting minutes fit for purpose? If not, or you don't know, what's your next step?

I got so nervous, that I skipped over the rules.

What can cause you to get nervous at meetings? What might you do about that?

I believe in myself. Not fully yet, but enough to commit.

What do you believe about yourself regarding your ability to chair consistently fulfilling meetings?

Dakkc's Log: Second Enlighten Meeting

4-D date 72-33

Today, I was determined not to make the same mistakes twice. You know what they say, "Fool me once, shame on you; fool me twice, shame on me."

I had a pretty good agenda. It included the meeting's purpose along with vivid, descriptive words for each agenda item. I also recovered ground lost last time over rules and roles. I issued a draft before the meeting, and called it 'Our Success Contract'. I added it to the agenda as 'Agree the draft Success Contract, prepared by Dakkc'.

Jargon didn't catch me out. I'd asked Logic, as the longest-serving hero, to do us a list of jargon with an explanation of each term.

As we were leaving, Not-Committed challenged me: "No one else in Süperbania bothers with the hassle of trying to improve their meetings. After all, everyone knows what they are like." I disagreed.

Not to be put off, he encouraged me to concentrate on tekky stuff, like improving the *flux inverters'* efficiency; stuff that might score me more hero points with the Guardians. To him, I was wrong-headed, trying to improve something that can't be changed. He even threw in a comment about my renaming and my need to get a good super-ability. He was concerned that I shouldn't follow my family into heroic obscurity. He went on, "Many heroes that chair meetings don't like them and don't control them properly, and those who attend them expect them to be unfulfilling and wasteful. It's just the way it is. It's been like this for as long as we can remember, and will be like that forever more."

In my opinion, expecting is very different to preferring, so Not-Committed's view, even if he's right about Süperbania society, only strengthens me. I've resolved to keep evolving and bettering what I do in my meetings. It's important. I will become a most excellent and bodacious chair, even though for now, I feel inadequate. After all, having these feelings of excitement and nervousness is one way of knowing that you are truly alive. Just like having one of your brains removed for a detoxifying, knowledge-replenishing bath and valet at the local *cerebellum* servicing shop.

NDC guided me through some good points. He replayed the interaction with Higher-Grade, who was late again.

> Higher-Grade: Sorry I'm late, everyone. The usual *flux inverter* overload on the Citadel Express train.

> Me: Welcome, Higher-Grade. I understand. Please take your seat, and I'll catch up with you after the meeting. We are on agenda item number three.

I thought I did well to even have that conversation with Higher-Grade. I was as nervous as a male-praying mantis in the mating season. I made sure not to tell him off in

31

front of the other heroes. I didn't, however, excuse his behaviour either. Understanding is different from agreeing. I believe I got the balance right.

I should've kept the arrangement to speak with him after the meeting, though. Honestly, I was so nervous about challenging a senior person, that I probably conveniently forgot. NDC helped me clarify. There could be many reasons for Higher-Grade, or any participant, not being on time. It needn't be the reason I've deduced through my fear. I was assuming that he didn't see Enlighten as a valuable use of his time, or me as a capable chair, and that at any given moment he'd use his super-strength to squeeze me down to the size of an atom.

It's now too late to go and talk with Higher-Grade. I've put it down to experience, to learn from it and behave differently next time. NDC, though, shape-shifted into Higher-Grade so I could practice the conversation. It was just like the real thing.

> Me: Hi, Higher-Grade. I said I would pick up with you about your arriving late for our second meeting. I believe it's important that we start every meeting on time with everyone there. I'm curious about your being late for our first two meetings.
>
> NDC as Higher-Grade: Yes, sorry about that. It's the Citadel Express train. Guardian-run transport simply isn't reliable.
>
> Me: I totally get your complaints about Guardian-run services. We both know it's prone to delays;

but what might you do to make sure you arrive at our future meetings on time?

NDC as Higher-Grade: Well, I suppose I could get an earlier train.

Me: Okay; though it doesn't sound like you're fully behind that idea.

NDC as Higher-Grade: You're right; I'm not. It seems such as waste.

Me: How about we start all our future meetings thirty minutes later? That way, you can still get the same train and get to our Enlighten meetings comfortably on time.

NDC as Higher-Grade: Yip. That sounds great.

Me: Okay. I'll let everyone know, and thanks for working with me on this. I appreciate it.

NDC praised my active listening. He said I showed promise as a coach. That felt good.

He and I then looked at what didn't go well. I could've made a better start. Confirming the meeting's purpose went okay, he went on to say that I'd used too many 'ehs', and sounded as non-assertive as a shy anthropophagic. Plus, I didn't outline the meeting. I fessed up to NDC that I remembered afterwards that Master Al Geon had said something to me, in yet another thought-call, about walking through the agenda. It lets people know the types of contributions that you're looking for, and highlights items that need decisions, and those for discussion and sharing. Apparently, it helps participants prepare for the coming agenda. It would also help settle me into the meeting, because I can rehearse much of it in advance. I ought to be less nervy as a result.

Something that took me by surprise was rehashing old decisions. At the first meeting, we agreed to use the Blue Planet's timescales. We agreed touchdown on 00.01 on 1 April GMT. "Job done," I thought. "Move on." Who was I kidding? Details reopened the issue under 'Any Other Business'. Before I knew it, Details and Hidden-Agenda were off again. I felt a sense of *Sonzi Day*, as we replayed our first meeting seemingly word for word. So surreal was it, that I began to wonder if NDC was up to his old video play-back in real time again. It's clear that revisiting decisions is a danger in meetings, and so I'll be ready for it in future.

Later, reading some of Jemst's Blue Planet research, I found reference to 'Group Memory' in meetings. It involves putting decisions and key points onto flipchart paper or similar, and displaying them at all meetings. Showing the data as a 'Group Memory' helps avoid wasting precious time rehashing old decisions. Whatever is flipchart paper? I may just add all agreed decisions to our future agendas.

Where I nearly came unstuck, was agreeing our Success Contract. It started with silence when I asked for comments. Within seconds, we seemed to be reliving the Synth wars, as Creative and Logic got animated. Speech-

Maker then began to make a point, but lacking any substance, she progressed to reasoning without focus, and ended up altering her physical form to liquid before evaporating into a cloud of steam.

On reflection, I ought to have spoken with some, or all, of the participants before the meeting. I could have asked Builder to make a positive comment to start us off, Higher-Grade for his support, and Details to give me her concerns (to help me prepare). Jemst called it lobbying. It's a fundamental activity for the effective chair.

I got a Success Contract agreed, though it took longer and used more emotional energy than needed. This was regardless of us having to rescue Speech-Maker from the air-cooling system as she rematerialised into her solid form. The upside, though, is that we have a Success Contract. It's done. Agreed. I've established these meeting behaviours, and I'll make sure we all follow them. They'll not just gather metaphorical dust.

Lastly, getting the right types of contribution remains a problem. As chair, I accept responsibility for that. I play the biggest role in creating the conditions for great meetings.

Details, for example, took us deeply into the minutiae of solar inversion displacement. At best, it's mildly interesting to a 4-D travel geek; at worst, it's a complete distraction. Next Not-Committed got off his chest how badly a previous project treated him, and Speech-Maker ended up as a puddle on the floor—twice. She gives speeches instead of punchy, accurate, and valuable comments targeted at the agenda item in question. In the meeting, I realised that if I gave Speech-Maker eye contact, I'd be dead. Or, more accurately, dead likely to get a four-minute lecture on some tangent subject, followed by either a messy floor or a blocked air-cooler.

For the entire second half of the meeting, I didn't look at Speech-Maker. That's not fair to her, me, or the project. I will need to act, but I'm just not sure how yet.

Overall, I'm feeling a little better about the future. I've still many doubts, though. Meetings will remain tough for me. My resolve's intact, and I've got an emerging thought-through plan of action for meeting three. Think, Plan, Do; Think, Plan, Do; Think Plan Do.

Your reflections

I had a pretty good agenda. It included the meeting's purpose along with vivid, descriptive words for each agenda item.

> Do your agendas state the meeting's purpose and use descriptive words in every agenda item? If not then what's your action?

In my opinion, expecting is very different to preferring.

> What do your participants expect will happen at meetings? How do you think they feel about them? Would they prefer a different experience? If so, what could be a first action step?

Jemst called it lobbying. It's a fundamental activity for the effective chair.

> How might you improve your lobbying beforehand to get the best from your meetings?

Dakkc's Log: The stroll
4-D date 72-40

Jemst and I visited the arboretum. As we enjoyed our stroll, avoiding the fragrant yet poisonous *clarp*, the conversation turned to meetings.

I updated her about my actions before and during my second meeting. I felt this meeting was better, although it could have been better still. I'm still nervous, and use lots of energy chairing, but I suppose I'm getting there slowly.

Jemst observed that I looked more confident as I spoke about this second meeting. It's true; I'm proud of myself for building on the first one. Jemst overheard in the central dining hub, that some participants really valued the jargon buster. Apparently, they too, didn't know some of the acronyms and terminology, but didn't like to ask!

She says that on the Blue Planet, the chair person can have different titles—names like host, facilitator, chair, convenor, lead person, manager, project leader, and so on. For me, the title doesn't matter. It's simply the role that's responsible for achieving the meeting's purpose.

It was then that I had a brainwave about roles. I realised that every participant at meetings ought to have a job to do. Giving the jargon buster to Logic fits with that idea. Jemst said that on the Blue Planet, 'participant' is a universal term for someone who attends meetings. In their dictionary 'participate' means 'be involved or take part'.

From today, everyone at my meetings will participate. It's amazing what comes to the surface when you walk and talk with friends.

As I glowed on the inside, Jemst brought me back to ground. She said that I'm not the finished chair yet. I must stay with the Think, Plan, Do mantra.

We parted with the edge off my inner glow and the realisation of the trials ahead. My thoughts turned to my up-and-coming conversation with Speech-maker.

Just as I was about to turn in for the night, Master Al Geon thought-called me again. It was nice of her, though it feels all too weird that our most supremest of beings still gets in touch. She offered me a tip that on reflection was really two tips. One was some research from *Thoth*. It says that the longer someone goes without speaking at a meeting, the harder it is for them to say anything. The Master encouraged me to make sure that everyone says something within the first minute or two of every meeting. She called them ice-breakers. I've no idea why she used that term, as our venues always maintain a pleasant temperature. Strange! What's also strange is that while Master Al Geon said I ought to do it, I had no inkling that she'd ever actually done it herself. I guess there is a difference between having knowledge and acting on it ... even for the most experienced and wise.

While staying hydrated with H_2O, I committed to enjoying the challenge of thinking up different short, yet interesting, ways of ice-breaking. After all, your name, your home world, and something unusual about your species' breeding habits is one that others use. I'll be different—better.

Master Al Geon then went on to tell me about transition. Heroes arriving at my meeting have come from doing something else. I, however, need them to be alert, aware, and ready to focus on what I need them to do ... to achieve our meeting's purpose. My participants may have just been in another challenging meeting (helping to save a universe from eradication by a rogue *Higgs boson* infestation), laundering their overpants, in a heavy ESP conference, in a disciplinary hearing, rushing from a transport hub, or having harsh words with their partner. Regardless, I need them to make the mental transition quickly, switching their focus from what they've been doing, to our meeting.

After some more H_2O, I figured the Master's two tips were one because the ice-breaker and the transition activity could be the same. That's even more efficient. I'll award myself a *Nike* star for that one, I think.

Time for bed.

Your reflections

Jemst overheard in the central dining hub, that some participants really valued the jargon buster. Apparently, they too, didn't know some of the acronyms and terminology, but didn't like to ask!

Most forums need a jargon buster. Think for a moment of all the jargon, 'insider language', and TLAs used in your meetings. (See what I did there?). Might you benefit from having one?

From today, everyone at my meetings will participate.

To what extent does everyone at your meetings have a role at every meeting? What's a potential next step for you?

It's amazing what comes to the surface when you walk and talk with friends.

> Could you and other chair people get together to improve things? How might you develop this as an idea?

The Master encouraged me to make sure that everyone says something within the first minute or two of every meeting.

> Is this an action for you?

I'll award myself a Nike star for that one, I think.

> How do you reward yourself for a job well done or a good idea?

Dakkc's Log: Meeting Speech-Maker

4-D date 77-89

I've got a week left before our third Enlighten meeting.

I must say that my recent dealings with Higher-Grade show that we've got an improving relationship. Maybe it's also because I spoke with him, albeit indirectly, about his arriving late. The bottom line is, I'm gaining his respect. I think.

I made a point of getting together with Speech-Maker today—an informal chat at StarCredits. Over a *Bian-5* latte, I fed back that I'd noticed her contributions were long, unstructured, and so lacked impact. I told her I had faith that she had much more value to offer. I wanted to help her.

Clearly, no one had spoken to her about this before. Initially defensive, she waivered on the point of liquidity, narrowly avoiding the indignity of a mop bucket. Hidden-Agenda rushed over from another table and resolidified her. With her cold-harnessing ability, she frostily stared her back to a solid.

I'm glad I'd anticipated some reaction from her. I was prepared. After a few moments, she opened up. She put it down to nerves, plus having a kind of random mind. Having three brains will do that to you, I suppose.

She agreed to set aside ten minutes for meeting preparation, to help distil her contributions. I agreed to help by mailing her beforehand with a list of the items I thought needed her expertise. When I wanted her contribution, I would use words like 'summarise', 'your top three points relating to ...', and other such terms to help focus her responses. I asked her to make eye contact with everyone, rather than just me, when speaking. And, of course, I promised to give her feedback afterwards. We left on good terms. I was thrilled when later in the day, Speech-Maker thanked me for taking the time to talk with her. She's promised to work hard to improve.

On my way home, I bumped into Creative on the express train. Well, she actually reversed her mobility chair over my foot! To be fair, it was a crowded carriage. She chatted about a timed agenda as a potentially splendid tool. She hadn't tried it but had read about it in a report some years ago. I thought the idea had merit too. As I wondered why she hadn't used it herself, the train abruptly jerked to a stop, and my attention jumped to survival mode. Creative engaged her super-stretch capabilities to wrap her arms in an all-too-complicated knot around a handrail, as passengers bumped and barged to get off.

With the evidence from Higher-Grade, Creative, and Speech-Maker, I have a growing sense that heroes take me more seriously—more of a hero, and less of an apprentice. Jemst, too, said I'm more confident.

I'm cautiously optimistic about meeting three ... Think, Plan, Do; Think, Plan, Do; Think, Plan, Do.

Your reflections

I made a point of getting together with Speech-Maker today.

Who might you need to feedback to about their meeting performance? Have you conveniently deprioritised it? Here are a few pointers to help you prepare:

Who is it you want to speak with?

Situation: What specifically are they doing that needs to change. Use facts (for example, they've been late with seven out of their last eight actions).

Impact: What is the result of what they're doing? Use facts (for example, extra time needed chasing actions and potential project delays) and a genuine feeling (for example, letting them know that you are disappointed, angry, frustrated, let down, etc.).

45

Next steps: What do you want to see happening next? (For example, they should let you know as soon as they anticipate a problem with meeting a deadline.)

Think about how they might react, and plan what you will do about each scenario you think of.

Now you can have the conversation.

Dakkc's Log: Third Enlighten Meeting

4-D date 78-28

Today's third Enlighten meeting was another step in my improvement journey as chair hero. We're getting closer to Blue Planet first contact, and edging nearer to my goal of hero status with, of course, my cape and powerful new name.

Having everyone speak in the first minute or so was a bit strange, but it worked. Everyone contributed. I also know that it helped people to park what was on their mind, and so concentrate on our meeting. I was on fire. Well, not physically of course (that's Builder's super-ability). I have *twaron* DNA, so am fire resistant anyway. What I mean is that my first few minutes were excellent. Higher-Grade arrived on time, everyone spoke within the first minute or so, and I walked through the agenda, giving a little insight into each item as I went along.

I positioned each new agenda item constructively, and emphasised the active word—the doing word, or the verb. Words like, 'decide', 'agree', 'share', 'present', 'discuss', 'problem-solve', 'create', 'generate', etc. This helped diffuse any tensions, and directed people's input. No point getting in a tizzy over an item that doesn't ask for a decision.

This probably won't mean anything to you but the word 'verb' in Süperbanian means a slimy fish with seven eyes—all of them crossed. It just makes me laugh every time I say it.

As we ended each item, I confirmed any actions. Specifically, who, would do precisely what, and by when.

I did, however, need to manage a situation with Not-Committed. We were about halfway through the meeting when I realised that Not-Committed had refused (albeit politely) three suggested actions. At the time, I reckoned everyone else had at least four actions. So I said to Not-Committed, "I've noticed, Not-Committed, that this is the third time today you've rejected an action that the group feel is naturally yours. I am starting to wonder about that, especially as it's in our agreed Success Contract to accept a fair share of actions as part of a high-performing project team."

Well, you could have knocked him down with a feather. Out of the corner of my back-up eye, I sensed the others nodding at one another, as if to say, "Well done, Dakkc, for tackling Not-Committed." Anyhow, Not-Committed fumbled something like, "I am awfully busy just now, and you could argue that Details or Builder could take on the tasks suggested for me." As he spoke, he started shrinking.

Undaunted, I replied, "I appreciate you have other work commitments, but given Project Enlighten's importance, I could speak with your hero boss about your workload if you wish." He continued reducing in size. Somewhat anxious at this, but determined to make my point, I

48

continued, "In the meantime, I want you to take a fair share of the action points. May I count on you, Not-Committed, to do that from now on?"

Not-Committed completed our interaction with a yes. That was enough for me. By now, though, he was at risk of falling through a gap in the floorboards. Thankfully, within a minute he'd returned to normal.

Needless to say, Not-Committed took on several actions during the rest of the meeting. He hasn't yet asked me to intervene with his boss, and I don't expect he ever will.

I was so pleased that I'd persisted. Jemst called it assertive behaviour. I simply spoke about the situation factually, and stated what I wanted in an honest and direct way without violating his rights as a sentient being.

Another benefit of dealing with Not-Committed is that the others are increasingly responsive to me, and to my suggestions to increase our meeting performance.

It's not all rosy yet, though. I had other challenges that, if I'd had NDC's help beforehand, I could have avoided. It was the third meeting to overrun. I'm dismayed that as professionals we can't finish a meeting on time. I feel that we ought to be able to start and finish a meeting as planned. I mean, how hard can it be?

Master Al Geon bumped into me—another strange encounter—at our village sports day. During the final of target *harrouu*, she suggested putting times against each agenda item. It seemed too much of a cosmic coincidence that now two people have suggested it. I will definitely do it next time. I'm sure it will help me to manage the agenda and, therefore, the meeting; give participants a sense of each agenda item's relative importance; and give me opportunities to encourage and motivate as we progress through the agenda.

There is a risk, however, that I might use the times as I would a *Hadesian* straight-jacket, and not as a guide. I'll stay out of that trap.

There are other development areas for me to think about.

Firstly, to improve participants' contributions. I want meetings where everyone gives their talents and perspectives in making quality decisions.

Secondly, there were a couple of examples today where we fudged it. One of them was agreeing that our first Blue Planet contact broadcast will be in Rastafarian; not because it was a quality decision, but simply because we were impatient to move on. Later an item that was due for a simple discussion grew arms, tongues, and legs and seemed to go on forever.

Thirdly, I included an agenda item to review our performance and process. A library resource about successful meetings said this was a good idea. Unfortunately, the result, when I asked for ideas, was silence—and an uncomfortable silence at that.

When I talked things through afterwards with NDC, I realised something obvious: my heroes weren't used to being asked for feedback. Their unwelcome silence should have been as easy to predict as the outcome of the Déjà-vu Olympics on the *Tarot* system.

After mentally kicking myself over my naiveté, I've come up with several improvement ideas already. I could let them know in advance and then do some lobbying. I could also approach the agenda item as a paired or small group activity, as participants are more likely to suggest things if it's from a group. If some of their comments could be about me, I could even leave the room to grab a *Bian-5* latte while they get on with the activity.

I do wish a conversation with Details had gone a whole lot better. Using NDC's special abilities, I reviewed it.

> Me: Details, I want to speak with you about your contribution at meetings.
>
> Details (defensively): Uh-hu. What is it?
>
> Me: Well, I see you've a great strength for detailed analysis. You put things in such great perspective, which helps show the rest of us ways forward. That's vital to us in making clear decisions. However, yesterday you set out eight concerns without giving a suggestion for any of them. We must use your expertise to its best, so I want to see you follow up each of your concerns with a workable suggestion.
>
> Details: Crikey, I tell myself that I'm a hugely experienced hero whose super-capabilities help

lots of projects. I take pride in my abilities to see through solids—even something that's painted over in lead, wrapped in lead, encased in a lead box, and finally buried in a lead casket. The <u>tone</u> of what I'm <u>hearing</u> is that you don't want my input, especially if it's to <u>sound</u> <u>off</u> or raise <u>alarms</u> <u>bells</u>. And that I've got to be constantly <u>harmonious</u> instead. Remember, I'm a mere hero not a deity. Sometimes the answer won't have <u>clicked</u> into place for me, but at the same time <u>something will tell me</u> that it's relevant to <u>voice</u> my concern.

Me: Details, please let me <u>clarify.</u> I value all of your gifts highly. Please keep what I've said in <u>perspective</u>. Let me make myself <u>crystal clear</u>. I want to <u>see</u> suggestions follow your contributions, especially when you raise a concern. I can see that there may be the odd occasion when you must raise the point even if you've <u>drawn a blank</u> over what to do. However, I <u>view</u> these as odd occasions. My <u>focus</u> is that I want your considerable expertise, and it's simply good practice to <u>show</u> us possible solutions when you <u>highlight</u> a potential issue. Will you do that for me?

Details: Well, I suppose so. To be honest, something <u>tells me</u> that there is more <u>discord</u> here than you're letting on.

Me: Absolutely not. All I want is to see that your contribution is as solution focused as possible. It's my role as chair to support you in that. The Blue Planet First Contact Enlighten project is really important.

Details: Oh well then. Fair enough. I will do as you say.

I saw that, while I stayed assertive, which was great, we were out of rapport. I'm a good hero, as is Details. I confess that I did sense that our relationship was a bit off. Using NDC to go over the conversation again, confirmed the issue. I used lots of visual words, such as see, perspective, view, etc. Perhaps, deep down, I thought I was appealing to her special visual abilities. Details, however, used more hearing words, such as sounds, something tells me, clicked, etc. It all helps explain why I sensed that our rapport could've been better. We were talking a different language!

I will have to notice heroes' sensory preferences, and look into this area of communication more deeply.

Jemst, my trusty student of the Blue Planet, let me know that the 'mostly water beings' have a saying. They describe interpersonal challenges as 'We are not on the same wavelength'. They're right.

So it was a better meeting for me, but I fear I'm still not good enough. Just as my heroic status seems to be within my grasp, I discover more challenges and actions. I must Think, Plan, Do; Think, Plan, do; Think, Plan, Do.

Your reflections

I emphasised the active word—the doing word, or the verb. Words like, 'decide', 'agree', 'share', 'present', 'discuss', 'problem-solve', 'create', 'generate', etc.

How would you rate the quality of agenda item descriptions at your meetings? (Use one to ten, with ten being the highest.) Give yourself one improvement action.

As we ended each item, I confirmed any actions. Specifically, who, will do precisely what, and by when.

How well do your meetings clarify any actions needed before moving on? Is there a possible action here emerging for you?

Jemst called it assertive behaviour. I simply spoke about the situation factually, and said what I wanted honestly and directly without violating his rights as a sentient being.

> How do you rate your assertiveness capability? What might you do if you want to improve?

Not because it was a quality decision, but simply because we were impatient to move on.

> Is this an issue at your meetings? If so, what might you do to change it?

I'll notice heroes' sensory preferences.

> How well do you flex your communication to get the best from people? Make a point of noticing from today.

Dakkc's Log: Fourth Enlighten Meeting

4-D date 83-12

It's been great to see that some of our practice has become second nature to me and the team. It's such a good feeling. Perhaps I could bottle it and sell it. Maybe at the annual convention on 'Negative emotions to self-motivation in a universe that no longer cares'. That's if anyone bothers to turn up this year.

Remembering Jemst and my Think, Plan, Do mantra before the meeting, I thought about how each agenda item might unfold. This helped me plan how to deal with each scenario I'd imagined. It's like your own 4-D movie without the noisy *Dimrain* popcorn crunchers behind you. I'm happy with my lobbying beforehand too.

Everyone contributed early on, and I walked through the agenda painting a vivid picture of each item. Before finishing each discussion, I clarified actions and always positioned each new item constructively.

I'd looked at some simple facilitation tools for ways to get participant contributions. I used them to help us explore a topic, generate ideas, and ultimately make decisions. These helped me fantastically well. I'll look out for more of these techniques and create my own library.

I'm also proud of a technique I created myself. Opening an agenda item, I said I would first take comments from the north of the room, then the east, and then west. One result was that Speech-Maker's opportunity came only after others had had theirs. Varying the approach to items really worked for me today.

I've got a niggling feeling, like the gnawing in your tummy telling you that you need some proteins. I realise that I'm doing too much. I haven't actioned my earlier insight about every participant having a role at every meeting. I'll arrange it now—even if it's to bring the *Palioxian* lamb sandwiches.

For one agenda item, I wanted the freedom to contribute, so I asked Creative to be the chair for that item. Confusion ensued. I wasn't in any way asking Creative to empathise with her mobility aid; I just needed to explain the term 'be the chair'. Once clarified, she was fine and did a good job. I was free to participate fully in that item using all the processing power of my three brains.

I still can't believe that Not-Committed sent a 'subby' (a substitute), who didn't have the authority to make decisions. ARRGGGGHHHH! Fortunately, I could delay the decisions we had today without affecting Enlighten's critical project path. But it was a valuable lesson for me. I'll make sure that this will not happen again by:

- Updating our Success Contract with our protocol for sending substitutes

- Adding 'Decision-making meeting' to the top of future agendas that include vital decisions items
- Thought-calling all essential participants as part of my meeting preparation when we are to make big decisions.

Returning to the upsides from today, I ran a short group exercise to help us review our meeting process. This generated a couple of improvements, such as sending out the minutes within forty-eight hours. So far, it's been the night before the next meeting.

We talked about moving the meetings around to different citadel locations. The rationale was that the same people travel across the citadel for every meeting, so varying the venue seemed fairer.

I went with the venue suggestion as long as it wouldn't interfere with something Master Al Geon told me on her most recent "just passing through" thought-call. Why IS she still so interested in me? It's starting to get to me. Anyway, she mentioned anchoring. (Anchor means the same in both Süperbanian and the Blue Planet's English. Maybe it has something to do with the original Star Travellers, of whom it's fabled would often 'anchor' their vehicles on planets with good natural resources. Who knows? It's just interesting.)

Anyway, if we had a super-productive meeting in the Vega room then I would book the Vega room for our next meeting. Why? Because the good vibes of productivity are anchored in that room. So when we arrive for the next meeting, we can get off to a great start because of what's anchored there.

And, of course, the opposite is true. If we have a grumpy, strained, emotionally charged, difficult meeting in the Callisto room, with puddles on the floor and participants disappearing through floorboards, then there is no way on Süperbania that I'll have the next meeting there—even if it's the only free room in the citadel.

It all makes sense, which proves that sometimes you should heed the advice from elders like Master Al Geon.

It struck me that I ought to let the project team know how I thought we were progressing. Not-Committed and Details, especially, deserve to know how I've found their performance since our chats.

So, to the team, I finished the meeting with something more than the ritual "Thanks everyone". I found giving positive comments easy. What surprised me was drying up and shying away from getting specific over what I felt we could improve. I was like the bi-annual solitary raindrop landing on the molten desert of *Vindaloo-8*.

I've since concluded that it was an internal dilemma. Not a thinking one that we sometimes get from our three brains, but more a guts-feeling dilemma. It centred on knowing which of my developmental feedback was for everyone, and which was for particular heroes. I asked myself, "Am I trying to sneak individual comments under the guise of saying them to everyone?" For example, I mumbled that I looked forward to everyone doing the appropriate amount of preparation for future meetings. Actually, I needed a one-to-one conversation with Hidden-Agenda. She's twice come unprepared for vital topics.

I've also realised that I didn't prepare what I was actually going to say. I am kicking myself, as, by now, I ought to know that everything I can prepare in advance, I should. No excuses. It is firmly down to me.

The individual positive feedback was much better. I made sure to bump into Details and let her know how valuable her contribution was. And here's how I delivered it: "Details, I wanted to specifically take some time to tell you how much I valued all of your contributions at today's Enlighten meeting. I noticed that all seven of your major contributions caused the team to think deeply about your possible solutions. Thanks. I appreciate it."

With Not-Committed, I took a similar fact-based approach. Shame I couldn't do it in person. The Guardians seconded him to locate an errant Truth Quark, so he'd temporarily shrunk to the size of a super-accelerated proton particle. I thought-called him instead.

After speaking to Jemst, I recognised that I could've improved the agenda's order. In future, where I can manage it, I'll deal with easy items at the start. It'll warm heroes up to the meeting and help them get into the flow. As Jemst said, "At The Cosmic Friendly Games, sprinters don't just turn up and run galaxy record-breaking times— they warm up first. It's the same with meeting participants." I think this approach will also help team motivation. I'll put the more taxing items in the middle of the agenda, and things to look forward to at the end.

Hands up. I definitely used the agenda timings as a *Hadesian* straight-jacket. I remember, for example, saying to the participants things like, "We only have two minutes left." I could've kicked myself, as I didn't want to fall into that trap.

NDC inspired me with the simple question: "How much time do you spend preparing for your meeting's end compared to the meeting's start?" It was like he'd opened a shiny new window in my meeting skills' soul. I admitted that I now spend a lot of time on a meeting's start but little or no time preparing for a meeting's end. When NDC asked me the implications of this, I was able to tell her that:

- Beings remember the beginnings and ends of things, whether a 4-D movie, a presentation, or a meeting; and that I should make each of them quality
- Ending a meeting as well as I start it says something about my capability and, therefore, enhances my reputation. Build the Dakkc brand, in other words.

NDC asked me if there was anything else that I might consider doing differently. It struck me that I should have mentioned the '*Ecto-couplings*' item due at our next meeting. It's a mission- critical item, and I ought to have made sure that the project team had plenty of warning—

well, not so much warning more like time for the issue to sink into their subconscious. In doing so, it would help them prepare. I mailed them to fix it. In future, I will add positioning (or is it positing?) an important item for the following meeting to my end-of-meeting routine.

Overall though, we were more active this time. That's good. Even though there are still improvements, both Creative and Logic, on their way out, said, "That was a productive meeting. Thank you." I thought, "Wow! An actual compliment from such experienced heroes." For a brief moment, I could feel that cape—MY CAPE—fluttering around my shoulders. What a glorious warm feeling.

I'm still not content. My final reflection is that I don't feel I have a large enough stock of simple meeting facilitation tools and techniques ... yet.

Your reflections

I thought through how each agenda item might unfold.

> How much time do you invest thinking through a meeting beforehand? What benefits would you get from doing this?

Varying the approach to items really worked for me today.

Could you use more varied ways to encourage your participants to contribute? If yes, when might you start?

I still can't believe that Not-Committed sent a 'subby' (a substitute).

To what extent are substitutes, especially ones that come without the authority to make decisions, infecting your meetings? What could be a next step for you?

I ran a short group exercise to help us review our meeting process.

> When might you do a simple group exercise to review your meeting's process and outcomes?

It struck me that I ought to let the project team know how I thought we were progressing.

> When might you next give quality feedback to your meeting participants?

NDC inspired me with the simple question: "How much time do you spend preparing for your meeting's end compared to the meeting's start?"

> How would you answer NDC? What could be an action step for you?

Dakkc's Log: Fifth Enlighten Meeting

4-D date 87-27

I was rockin' at today's Enlighten meeting. My 'prep' included asking Hidden-Agenda to suggest and facilitate our starting transition activity. It was quite an ask. She is more used to her super-gift of producing a frosty atmosphere, colder than a Blue Planet polar bear with alopecia. But it meant that she and Not-Committed, the two who participate the least, have done the meeting start-up activity. In my welcome, I reminded everyone of one point in our Success Contract. I want our contract always in our minds. I'm basically reinforcing that I don't care how incompetent other heroes may be at running meetings—our meetings are going to be great for everyone.

I used agenda timings a lot better today. At the start of each item, I told everyone how long we planned to spend on it, but at the same time, I didn't get hung up about time passing. At the last meeting I must have come across like the compulsive overeating *hippo-rocerous* of *Limos* at ten minutes past dinner time. Today, I waited till we were halfway through our agenda, then I let everyone know how pleased I was that we were having a quality, on-schedule meeting. This gentler use of the timings was how NDC had experienced it working on his home world.

An hour into our meeting, it was obvious that a fifteen-minute item needed longer. We were uncovering good stuff that we simply needed to talk through. I offered the meeting a choice. I estimated the item was worth another thirty minutes, which meant either dropping one or more other items and finishing on time or extending the meeting by thirty minutes. To my surprise, we quickly reached an agreement. We dropped one fifteen-minute item and had the meeting finish fifteen minutes after the original published time, so we still finished on a mutually-agreed revised time. In the team's eyes that was still a win.

I'm convinced that highlighting the '*Ecto-couplings*' agenda item after our last meeting gave us a better discussion about it today. Very pleasing.

I don't believe that anything went badly today. It was simply an effective meeting. Some things went really smoothly while others had their moments. Overall, we met our purpose and objectives on our agreed timescale. Details, Creative, and Logic said afterwards that they now enjoy attending my meetings, as "we get things done" and "they're not boring". They're usually frustrated in meetings; often thinking they could be doing something else more productive—like a *Hephaestusian* post-it note inventory.

Without prompting, NDC asked to show me part of my after-meeting conversation with Hidden-Agenda. Here's how it went:

> Me: Hidden-Agenda, I noticed that when we discussed the Blue Planet landing module

fabrication, you made the case for *yugs*. Yet we decided at meeting two that we'd make it from the lighter *krink*. I'm curious about that.

Hidden-Agenda: Well I still think *yugs* because its camouflage properties are more reliable. That will help <u>avoid</u> detection by the 'mostly water beings'. We've all seen the video of transportation vehicles stripped bare and propped up on bits of masonry when they're left stationary down there. It's a fate we must protect our craft against. It will also help <u>fix</u> the manifold connection problems our technicians raised. Plus, it would mean us <u>not having to</u> waste time with additional quality assurance. *Yugs* therefore <u>eliminates</u> several problematic issues for the project.

Me: I understand all of that, Hidden-Agenda, though none of these points are new ones. We decided on *krink* because it's lighter and has greater flexibility under stress. It'll help us <u>achieve</u> smoother landings and take-offs, plus <u>enable</u> us to anchor in any of the Blue Planet's environmental conditions. *Krink's* availability means that we'll get much quicker access to supplies and, perhaps most importantly, deliver the <u>benefit</u> of staying within budget. The Guardians and Master Al Geon herself are resolute about the Blue Planet first-contact trip needing to <u>attain</u> its objectives on budget.

Hidden-Agenda: I do see that, and yet *yugs* will help <u>prevent</u> many project risks. I ask you to add a review of the *krink* decision to the next agenda so that we can all discuss it.

Me: I see no new grounds for reviewing the *krink* decision. In fact, I'm convinced that its <u>advantages</u> overpower *yugs*'s on all our agreed key-decision criteria. I am wondering if your brother's ownership of the biggest *yugs* mine this side of Janus-Major is influencing your tenacity with this.

Hidden-Agenda: Indeed it is not. And I resent your implication. I just want the project to <u>stay out</u> of problems.

Me: Hidden-Agenda, I'm sorry if I've offended you. That wasn't my intention. I just see *krink* as ticking all the boxes necessary for us to <u>achieve</u> success. I'm still confused about what leads you to return, for a third time, to something the project team decided several meetings ago.

Hidden-Agenda: Well okay, *krink* it is; though I will still mail you with my arguments for *yugs*."

Me (trying out my studies on Blue Planet dialects): Okay, I'm cool with that.

When NDC highlighted certain words, it was easy to see what was going on. I am more motivated towards things and so use words like 'achieve' and 'benefit'. Hidden-

Agenda seems more motivated to get away from things and so uses words like 'prevent' and 'fix'.

So, while I'm still proud of my assertive behaviour and my calmness under pressure, I should have picked up on Hidden-Agenda's motivations and flexed how I'd had the conversation with her.

Looking at the conversation again, there's an argument for not mentioning Hidden-Agenda's brother owning a *yugs* mine. Sometimes it'll be right to not express a potential ulterior motive. This time we were at an impasse, so on balance it was useful to voice it. The effect was both of us knowing it as a piece of data. It was out in the open. In the machinations of project life, he knows that I know that his brother has a *yugs* mine, and I know that he knows that I know that his brother has a *yugs* mine. Oh, my brains hurt!

Sometimes, a nod really is as good as a wink to an *Aergian* bat with vision challenges! Something like that anyway.

It's rare for NDC to come straight out and tell me something, so it was particularly pleasing when he asserted that he now sees me as an adding-value hero. Like many heroes, I can reflect on key experiences. However, I can also celebrate what I do well and review what I could do better. Crucially, I've shown that I apply my actions to achieve improvements. That makes me an adding-value hero.

I know I said there wasn't really anything that went badly this time. Being super-critical, the meeting went on for too long without a break. I asked Master Al Geon's advice. She said that any meeting over ninety minutes ought to have a planned break so that heroes can hydrate, stretch, and re-energise themselves—Creative needs to stretch anyway after a while. Al Geon's experience was that it never happens even though the reasoning is sound enough. I used some of NDC's methods on Master Al Geon. I asked her what she thought led chair heroes to not use breaks in longer meetings. She looked like I'd caught her out. I didn't pursue it. I've deduced it's because chair heroes settle for the way things are. Most chairs don't factor in breaks in longer meetings, and the pressure to conform is so great that everyone just complies.

Because of my increasing confidence, I am going to put a ten-minute break into all agendas over ninety minutes. I can always negotiate the break away or have a few shorter, perhaps three-minute, energisers that achieve the same end—a re-energised group.

Actually, now that my meetings are going well, I have another niggling feeling like an itch that even Creative couldn't reach. It's the feeling that our meetings will become rituals as my current interesting things become normal. All my good practice will turn bland, and so lose its power. I've resolved that in addition to building my toolkit of simple facilitation tools and techniques, I need to do things to stop my meetings becoming stale. I mentioned the latter point to Father. Mistake. I had to endure a torturous lecture about avoiding staleness. Less yeast, and wrapping everything in aluminium foil was the summary.

Finally, remembering 'anchors' because it was such a good meeting, I will book this room for our next one.

Grumbs! I almost forgot Speech-Maker. As is now my normal practice, I sat down for feedback with Speech-Maker. I took a different approach this time. I asked her to tell me how she had gotten on at the meeting. She was tougher on herself than I would've been. I took the opportunity to help her rejoice in her progress and inject some proportion into what she saw as her 'disasters'. She, like NDC with me, ended by confirming her specific actions for our next meeting.

All this must take me a big step closer to the cape and hero status I've longed for all of my physical existence—and one step further away from my father's chosen title for me. Mum let me know today that he put me down for the recently vacant 'Profiteroleman' position. Gutted.

Your reflections

In my welcome, I reminded everyone of one point in our Success Contract. I want our contract always in our minds.

> Even if you don't yet have a Success Contract or similar, what would it take for you to remind people of one meeting behaviour at the start of each meeting? Do it.

I should have picked up on Hidden-Agenda's motivations and flexed how I had the conversation with her.

> What might you do to pick up on people's motivations?

Asserted that he now sees me as an adding-value hero.

> Who do you have that will feedback, challenge, and encourage you to improve your meetings?

Master Al Geon said: Any meeting over ninety minutes ought to have a planned break.

> What's your view of scheduling breaks into your meetings that are over ninety minutes?

I need to do things to stop my meetings becoming stale.

How might participants describe their experience at your meetings?

What's a next potential step for you?

Dakkc's Log: Sixth Enlighten Meeting

4-D date 91-35

Today I chose to remind my meeting heroes about the part of our Success Contract headed, "Attract my attention when you want to speak and I promise I will bring you in". I did this, as I knew agenda item number seven, 'Deciding who will go to the Blue Planet', would be emotive. We simply cannot take every hero.

I experimented with introducing differences by having different people chair different items. Good in principle, but I made another school-hero error—I didn't let the participants know in advance. Some said they would have wanted to prepare. Fair point. It shouldn't have happened. After all, I did the same thing to Creative at an earlier meeting.

I'd previously learned from Jemst's Blue Planet project that the best 'mostly water being' leaders are authentic, so I apologised. I explained my logic behind the experiment (keeping meetings lively and so avoiding staleness—more aluminium, less yeast). I confirmed I'd do it differently in the future. The team accepted the need to keep our meetings fresh, and it was just that my process was faulty ... this time.

I used two simple facilitation tools this time. One to help generate ideas, and the other to help us make a decision.

I'm pleased that my library of simple tools and techniques is evolving nicely.

I felt our meeting review went better this time; mainly because I gave plenty notice. I'd say that we are more of a high-performing heroic team now. That's because we dealt with this item as a round-table discussion. We shared openly and assertively our thoughts and observations on our processes and productivity.

Nothing went badly, aside from the usual, 'Any Other Business' (AOB). It's a time drain. Why is it that we do well, keep to time, and then AOB derails us? It's like we have meeting guerrillas, lying in wait for AOB to launch their topic grenades. One hero, who shall remain nameless, swung back in his chair and uttered, "I was just thinking as the meeting progressed, that we really ought to discuss the amount of glucose in the coffee replicator." Or, as happened last time, a hero proposed an array of rowdy and exotic pleasure planets for the end-of-Project-Enlighten jamboree. When these derailments happen, the floodgates open and time escapes as quickly as oxygen from a spacecraft punctured crossing the ice debris around *Ichee-Alpha*, and I get frustrated. And we overrun!

I was encouraged, therefore, when Builder sought me out after our meeting. She heralded her arrival with much flame; that's her way when she's excited. She had an idea to rid ourselves of AOB hijacks. Perhaps she could've said backdraughts! She entertained me with a story from a 4-D movie she'd watched the previous evening called 'What Every Hero Wants'. She really needs to get out more.

Anyway, she spoke of a meeting scene where the chair asked for any last-minute vital items at the start. Amazing. Once the chair had the items, she triaged them there and then. Some she added to the agenda, some she added to a future agenda, and some she dropped. It all worked amazingly well in 4-D movie land. I thanked Builder very much. I'll do some of my own research. As I considered seeking a thought-call with Master Al Geon, she thought-called me! Too weird. She confirmed that some planetary Guardian councils do the same at their meetings. They say it helps them manage 'Any Other Business', and better assures them of finishing on time.

As I hydrated on H_2O, I believe I've created the conditions for performance in my meetings. It showed in the way that we all behaved today. Creative spoke with me afterwards about lots of ideas for changing meetings and for keeping participants interested. I'll review them all and give her feedback. I need to balance freshness with change for changes sake. Jemst and I think Süperbanians are like 'mostly water beings'. We, too, need some unusualness and variety to keep us interested, but we also need customs for stability—like our festive gatherings, where families meet to exchange items of gaudy and unwearable knitwear.

I'm looking forward. I'm enthusiastic about meeting seven. It's our final one. I'm motivated and full of confidence. I've lots of thoughts about how to make sure the Enlighten project planning finishes on a high.

It's as if I've become as natural to chairing meetings as the evening solar lights in the *Clotho* system. I just hope I'm doing enough to secure the cape of my dreams. For me, for my family, and for my future descendants.

Your reflections

Jemst's Blue Planet project showed that the best 'mostly water being' leaders are authentic.

What does authentic leadership mean for you in your meetings?

I'm pleased that my library of simple tools and techniques is evolving nicely.

When might you commit to starting to build your library of simple tools and techniques for meetings? Where might you find them? Who might help you?

Why is it that we do well, keep to time, and then 'Any Other Business' derails us?

Are you plagued with 'Any Other Business' (AOB) hijacks? What's a possible solution for you?

If not AOB, what contaminates your meetings? What action could you take?

Dakkc's Log: Seventh Enlighten Meeting

4-D date 95-20

Our seventh meeting was my ideal of good-meeting practice. I lobbied beforehand, had a quality agenda, and I made sure everyone had a role. I prepared everyone for success by starting on time, regardless of who was there (they were all there by the way). Hidden-Agenda ran a good transition activity, and I signposted the meeting's agenda and reminded us of one Success Contract ingredient. We had the meeting in the same room as meeting six because that was such a good one.

It was my first time using, 'Any Last-Minute Vital Items' at the start instead of 'Any Other Business' at the end. It worked like a *Demeterian* charm. I understand now why Builder described it as triaging items. It's just like arriving at a sickbay emergency room. The clinician quickly assesses your symptoms to decide who will attend to you and when. Do you need a surgeon's expertise or the best guess of an overtired locum, awake only because of copious amounts of ingested *Bian* caffeine?

As I'd predicted, Hidden-Agenda, Not-Committed, Details, and Speech-Maker all had suggestions. I triaged them all quickly. Three of the four were not for our meeting, so I assigned them to our next pre-meeting discussion, known as 'coffee and gossip'. Only the fourth one was worthy of discussion. We gave it ten minutes.

Logic and Higher-Grade agreed to take five minutes off one of their agenda items, meaning that we still planned to finish on time. It really works this triaging of 'Any Last-Minute Vital Items'.

I feel that I facilitated the discussions particularly well by using simple tools to get contributions, generate ideas, and make decisions. I had to manage some more emotional hero issues, especially at item four: To agree who gets window seats on the trip. It's confirmed to me that you must have a decision process, be seen to be fair, and demonstrate assertive behaviour and decisiveness when required.

Emotions were still at play, and we had some heated debates. After all, it was for the best seats on a first-contact mission. However, our conflict was constructive, and because everyone had their say, I saw that they all committed to the recommendations I'll propose to the Guardians.

I experimented with having one participant's role— Builder—to summarise the actions at the end. I'll keep doing this, as it helped everyone to get, or ask for, clarity over our actions.

I made sure that our meeting had a quality finish to match our quality start. As it was our final meeting, we enjoyed a special *Rullaween* cake with our project name iced on top. Father excelled himself. It went well with a small *Pratsis* whisky and some relaxing fellowship. We shared some Project Enlighten memories, including Speech-Maker and Not-Committed   re-enacting   their   'hot-air'   and 'disappearing' acts, much to the amusement of the group. It was a splendid way of rounding off a splendid project.

When every hero had left, Speech-Maker approached me. The Guardians have asked her to chair a forum exploring the mythical origins of tummy fluff. She wants me as a mentor. I felt so good, that I've had the urge to smile for a full eight hours afterwards. Of course I'll help her. We simply must share and help everyone have consistently effective meetings.

NDC asked me to think about the benefit of all of my passage project efforts. Great question. After a moment, I began by noting that we had not needed the originally planned eighth meeting. Then I reflected that, although Süperbanian meetings tend to overrun by thirty percent, after meeting five, ours didn't.

I know in my hearts that our meetings were effective. We had fewer circular discussions, wasted contributions, and rehashing of old decisions. We had numerous simple ways for generating ideas and making decisions. I know the team are using the methods I introduced in their meetings—making sure, of course, that what they do fits their local culture. I've had plenty of informal feedback telling me how fulfilling our meetings were. Although I can't give it a star-credit value, it's good to know.

As for the benefits to me, I've developed skills that will help me way beyond meetings; skills like objective-setting, influencing, facilitating, coaching and mentoring, planning, reflective practice, and many more.

Prompted by NDC's question, I quickly thought-called the team a questionnaire about our meetings. I wanted to quantify their feedback. Most important was a simple question about our meetings' effectiveness. My average was eighty-six percent, compared to twenty-eight percent in the usual Süperbanian meetings. That's a fifty-eight percent difference—cause for a planetary celebration in many star systems.

At face value, my results are impressive, causing me to ponder about the impact if replicated across Süperbania. The potential benefit in time and star-credits is breathtaking, causing you to activate your back-up blood oxygenating synthetic chromosome!

I've decided to give a short benefits presentation for Master Al Geon and the Guardians. We shall see what happens. I hope it will get their tongues wagging. I'll be very nervous because the stakes are so high for me. I need to feel the fear and just do it.

My chief personal actions are to keep my meeting skills laser sharp by continuing to develop what I Think, Plan, and Do, and find ways of setting out the value that consistently effective meetings can deliver. Other than that, I await my fate. I've done my best. It's now up to the Guardians.

Your reflections

It's confirmed that you must have a decision process.

> How well to you use clear decision-making processes when you have decision items in your meetings?

As it was our final meeting, we enjoyed a special Rullaween cake with our project name iced onto it.

> How do you round off a series of meetings in a purposeful way to help people celebrate and move on with a good feeling?

Prompted by NDC's question, I quickly thought-called the team a questionnaire about our meetings. I wanted to quantify their feedback.

What stops you from surveying your meeting participants?

Find ways of setting out the value that consistently effective meetings can deliver.

How much time might you save if your whole organisation has consistently effective meetings? Do a quick, rough-and-ready calculation?

Dakkc's Log: Renaming
4-D Date 04-55

It's now four months since Project Enlighten wrapped up.

Today I got my cape and full hero status. I'm over the moons. I'm also relieved that I've avoided the family's 'Profiteroleman' renaming that awaited my failure. I didn't just get a regular hero cape, I got a special one, as the Guardians decided I'd done such a special job. It's self-cleaning with night lights, and it has both invisibility capability and H_2O protection. All my Project Enlighten colleagues and Master Al Geon endorsed me because of the project outcomes and that my contribution to meeting practice could have universal implications.

Some of my peers congratulated me and wanted to know more about my meeting practice. Others, as you can imagine, were more cynical about the kudos I received. One friend maintained that I was lucky. Apparently I had 'nice' heroes and the Blue Planet was an easy project. Before I had a chance to comment, Jemst leapt to my defence. She put him firmly in his place with a reference to the lack of multi-functionality on any of his family's capes.

Master Al Geon took me aside. She explained how I had fulfilled an ancient Star Traveller prophecy. A heady mix of legend, myth, and folklore foretelling that an apprentice from a line of under-heroic families would cure the disease of wasteful meetings.

It all makes sense now. Why Master Al Geon showed such unusual interest in me throughout the project, why I had this yearning to succeed, and why I persevered when many encouraged me to give up and accept the meetings status quo.

I'm in such demand as a meeting chair that I need to be wary of being typecast. It's bad when you get offered so much of the same thing to do. It's like you're punished for being skilled. Also, I now lead a team of heroes, so will have regular team meetings too. All the meeting principles are the same, of course.

We were going to call them Dakkc Meetings, but in the end, the Guardians decided on SÜPERB meetings Jemst said the 'mostly water beings' would understand this word and so be more likely to strive to achieve SÜPERB meetings

A SÜPERB meeting is one that attends to these six elements:

S   Set everyone up for success
Ü   Über starts
P   Purposeful through the agenda
E   End as well as you started
R   Review process and performance
B   Beware staleness

I still have to pinch myself that the Guardians invited me to the Blue Planet trip to share Süperbania's most recent precious gift: effective and fulfilling meetings. What an adventure. Truly experiencing things is so different to just reading about them. The smell of Jasmine on a balmy evening will live with me forever, and I'd rather forget that the 'mostly water beings' conspire to deny huge swathes of their people from accessing clean H_2O. Jemst's right: a world of contradictions.

And my renaming was, of course, 'SÜPERBmeetingsguy'. Not as catchy as Profiteroleman perhaps, but I love it. Jemst, however, laughed and called me a hippy! I've no idea what she meant. Trust your friends, though, to bring you back to Süperbania with a friendly bump. It keeps your feet firmly on the ground—and not a bit like a big balloon in zero gravity.

NDC joked, "This whole thing has been one rite of passage for Dakkc, and one giant leap for meeting practice." He's never lost for a one-liner.

Inevitably, as this glorious day draws to its end, my thoughts turn to my father and his bread, and my grandmother and her…well, the less said the better. With a welling up in my tear ducts, I begin (in my mind) to share my success with them and all my family from generations past. I am, after all, the product of their endeavours and experiences.

Onwards and upwards.

Your reflections

One friend maintained that I was lucky.

Do you believe in luck? How does your belief help or hinder your performance?

A SÜPERB meeting is one that attends to these six elements:

S   Set everyone up for success
Ü   Über starts
P   Purposeful through the agenda
E   End as well as you started
R   Review process and performance
B   Beware staleness

How might you use the SÜPERB Meetings™ ingredients in your future? Think about what already works well for you and where you need to develop actions.

At www.robertsontraining.co.uk you can download a free useful checklist.

Dakkc's Log: Meetings Cured

4-D date 04-58

By the rings of Planet Prostrate, I almost forgot! Horseshoe crabs. After Olde Master Al Geon explained to me about the prophecy, I couldn't resist asking about her Horseshoe crabs references. Were they random senior hero moments or were they part of her subtle messing with my brains?

Horseshoe crabs, she reminded me, inhabit many planets and have remarkable attributes and properties. They've lived on the Blue Planet for some 450 million years, have compound eyes, blue blood, don't have haemoglobin, and they don't get cancer—once considered the primary threat to species of all planets, apart from rock salt if you happen to be a gastropod.

There was a time on Süperbania when we believed we couldn't cure cancer. These living fossils inspired us to keep going with such heroic tenacity that we did indeed find that elusive cure.

Olde Master Al Geon confessed that many, many beings on many, many worlds believe that they can't cure the dreaded ineffective meetings disease. She hoped that Horseshoe crabs offered an inspirational hope, nay, expectation that every being can cure ineffective meetings.

Our newly named SÜPERB meetings will be that cure plus the antidote for future generations.

I thought it was a bit of a weird analogy but hey-ho. She's right though. Ineffective meetings are a disease—a pandemic on some worlds. I know SÜPERB meetings has great potential.

Your reflections

To what extent do you accept that you can chair consistently effective and fulfilling meetings for everyone?

To what extent does your organisation show that it wants to achieve consistently effective and fulfilling meetings? Score from one to ten, with ten being high.

Moral

You know that business meetings the world over have a reputation for varying degrees of ineffectiveness. Dakkc approached them with naiveté. He saw them as a business activity you can either do well or do badly. The difference is that Dakkc didn't settle for ineffective meetings as a norm. This is doubly significant, as Dakkc got strong messages from his peers and his seniors that meetings couldn't be improved. Dakkc, though, persevered. He had a mission.

The SÜPERB news is that ineffective meetings are curable. Whether team, project, spur-of-the-moment, in person, or virtual it makes no difference; the principles are the same.

As creator of SÜPERB Meetings™ and this fable, I see it as the blind spot core skill. It doesn't have to be that way. I've conducted thousands of straw polls with business people in a range of sectors and countries. The message is as predictable as the *De-ja-vu Olympics* in this fable. Meetings are ineffective and the source of great frustration and waste. Everyone I've spoken to longs for their meetings to be fulfilling experiences.

It's taken me years to figure out the reasons for this global disease. Could it be that more senior people usually run them, and they are less likely to ask for support? Perhaps we don't enable participants to speak up about their meeting experiences. Perhaps we don't know what good looks like. Or maybe, like Dakkc's experience, there is a planet-wide conspiracy, albeit unintended, to settle for meetings being the way they are—an unsolvable business disease.

Sitting on a beach one day, I remembered an associate of mine whose business farms horseshoe crabs. As you've read, these critters have been around for millennia and have many interesting features. One of them is that they don't get cancer. I couldn't resist making room for them in this book.

Just as humanity will cure cancer, we can cure ineffective meetings as a business disease. Dakkc's SÜPERB Meetings™ approach was the spur for a new reality on Süperbania—and it will be, too, for our Blue Planet when we commit to and persevere to improve our meetings.

I encourage you to all to take inspiration from Dakkc's journey of change, resolve to achieve consistently effective meetings, and be a meeting hero. Everyone will love you for it. We'd love to be your guide, and support you to achieve your meeting ambitions.

www.robertsontraining.co.uk

Achieve your Meeting Ambitions

For more information on Derek Robertson and the team, contact Robertson Training:

Tel: 01786 447 548

Mobile: 07977 143 233

Email: Dakkc@robertsontraining.co.uk

Please visit our website at: www.robertsontraining.co.uk

There you can download a free useful checklist.

Derek loves to hear from readers. He especially likes to hear about meeting success stories, the simple tools and techniques to facilitate that work for you, and, of course, how you found this book.

His team can help you achieve your meeting ambitions by defeating the many villains that conspire to thwart good meeting practice. Your 3-step plan to results is super simple:

1. Get in touch

2. We do the heavy lifting

3. You see the benefits

Printed in Poland
by Amazon Fulfillment
Poland Sp. z o.o., Wrocław

63123411R00056